ACCOUNTABILITY

by

Nancy Maworise Phiri

ACCOUNTABILITY
Copyright © 2019 Nancy Maworise Phiri

ISBN: 9781092809504

Published by:
RMPublishers
Office 1, Izabella House
24-26 Regent Place
Birmingham
B1 3NJ
www.rm-pa.org
info@rm-pa.org

Dedication

This book is a special dedication to my mum, Naomi Nhari-Maworise, and my granddad Brigadier Jacob Nhari. My granddad was a Salvation Army Brigadier who I can truly say was an accountable father to his children and to us his grandchildren, as well as a true man of God. My granddad was greatly used of God; many were saved, delivered and healed through his ministry.

God rewarded him by blessing him with grand children who are used of God and are on fire for the Lord. My mum grew up under a great man and from hence taught us as a family to love the Lord. Most of all my mum taught us personal accountability as we grew up. She was an accountable person herself. I am who I am today because of my mum.

My mum went to be with the Lord on the 3rd June 2018. My dad went to be with the Lord in November 2016. He was a very strict but good dad. It took me years to understand that our dad was strict because he wanted to protect us from the world and see that we did well in life.

This book is also a dedication to my sister Senseni Maworise-Mangwiro, my brother Jeffrey Maworise, my cousin Patience Tugwete Mutsanga who is my accountability partner and also my supportive husband Joseph Phiri.

My special appreciation goes to my friend Sook-Yen Allen who literally pushed me to finish this book.

She would check on me to see how far I had gone and also pray for me.

I thank my accountability partner Patience for helping me stay focused. I thank my uncle Cecil, Minister Shumirai, Bianca, Lindie, Lucas and Amanda for helping me by encouraging me as I wrote this book.

Contents

Preface

This book will challenge you to be better at everything you do whether you are a parent, a child, a spouse, an employee, or an employer. This book is based on Romans 14:12 which says, "And so, each of us will give an account of ourselves to God." However, this book is not for people who are easily offended.

It is for people who are willing to be challenged to live better lives, people who are willing to be answerable for their actions or to at least try. This is a small book as I am just delivering God's urgent message to the church written to challenge a large spectrum of people both Christian and non-Christian alike.

For Christians, not only does it address Christian leaders such as bishops, apostles, pastors, teachers, evangelists, worship leaders, deacons, elders but it also challenges the ordinary Christian and non-Christians.

This book also challenges the corporate world and leaders of nations including presidents, prime ministers, cabinet ministers and so on. It is also meant to challenge parents, grandparents and spouses.

On the 20th April 2010, I had an open vision and Jesus talked to me about accountability. Early in 2011, God spoke to me around 4 am and told me to write a book about accountability as described by Him. God even gave me the specific chapters I was supposed to write about. I was quite concerned by the instruction as I had never written a book before and so I thought I would not be able to make it. What I did not realise is that when God gives you an assignment, He gives you divine ability to do it. Throughout the year, I did not even start the book until something happened on 28th February 2012.

I collapsed at work and a colleague dialed the emergency services and I was taken to hospital. Back in December 2011, after a simple but delicate hospital procedure, I picked up a hospital infection. Though I had so much pain here and there, I kept going on as normal not knowing I had a serious abdominal infection until I collapsed.

I later learned that only 10% of people in the world who have such an infection had survived. From my second week in hospital onwards, I could not eat or drink as I could not keep the food and drink down. Whilst I was in the hospital, I read the Word of God a lot and listened to podcasts and worship music.

Just the smell of food from the trolley in the corridor made me nauseous. By the end of the third week, I did not have the energy to even read the Bible, let alone concentrate. A lot of people far and wide were praying for me. Things took another turn during that week; my temperature spiked high so did my blood pressure.

Doctors used different antibiotics to treat the infection, but nothing seemed to be working. I had 2 consultants and many doctors filing into my room every day until I started losing count of the days. In all that, I did not know my situation was critical but what I knew was that the doctors kept changing antibiotics as my temperature was not going down. They seemed to have given up as they had tried their best.

I was getting very weak and unable to eat any food. I started giving up. When my husband came to see me one evening, I told him I was tired and could not do this anymore. I later learned my husband panicked (and called my sisters and brother to inform them I was giving up). They started encouraging me and making declarations over me.

The following morning, as I was just sitting on the bed telling myself I couldn't do this anymore; God spoke to me clearly. He told me that when I stand before him giving an account of my life, it will not only be about me being saved and having led hundreds of people to Christ, but it would also be about the assignments that He has given me to do.

He told me I was accountable for the message that He gave me in 2005; to tell women worldwide about 3 am- 4 am time of intimacy with Him. I had started very well then ended up changing the time to a time of intercession and intimacy contrary to God's instruction. To make matters worse, many women had responded to the message worldwide, but I was now misleading them. I realised I was not ready to face my God. God also reminded me that he had instructed me to write the book *Accountability* and after *Accountability* to write two more books whose titles He has already given me.

The realisation that I was not ready to stand before God shocked me. I staggered into my hospital bathroom and cried before the Lord. I shouted, "Devil, I will not die but I will live and do what God has instructed me to do!! Devil, I will not die but live and declare the goodness of the Lord". I kept making those declarations repeatedly. I learned weeks later that by this time, doctors had tried everything they could, and they had given up. Notwithstanding, we serve a God of second chances!

God heard my prayers and a day after making these declarations, a microbiologist who was passing by our hospital was told about my case and advised the doctors to inject the antibiotics straight into my abdomen since they were not working intravenously which they did.

It was very painful, and I screamed the ward down. The following morning my temperature and blood pressure had gone back to normal and I was on my road to recovery. One of the consultants who went on five days annual leave was literally shocked when he came back and found me sitting outside the bed in a chair. In his words, "Nancy, I never ever imagined I would see you sitting in a chair like that again". That's when I realised how much of a miracle this had been. I ended up spending a total of four months in hospital- went in end of February and came out the end of June. What a mighty God we serve. This experience changed the way I walk as a child of God.

Definitions:

Accountability is defined as:
1. the "quality or state of being held accountable,
2. an obligation or willingness to accept a responsibility, to account for one's actions" (Merrimack Webster dictionary).

Business dictionary.com defines accountability as
1. the obligation of an individual or an organisation to account for its activity,
2. accept responsibility for them and to discuss the results in a transparent manner. (Business dictionary .com). It is the act of taking ownership.

Accountability is an important principle that could be used to shape families, workplaces, churches, and governments. However, because most people avoid conflict and do not want to be confrontational, they do not want to hold people accountable for their actions.

Most people actually hate being held accountable. For example, some children do not want to be held accountable by their parents; some spouses do not want to be held accountable by their significant others, some employees do not want to be held accountable by their employers; team members do not want to be held accountable by their colleagues, church members do not want to be held accountable by their pastors, pastors do not want to be held accountable by their elders and deacons and governments do not want to be accountable to their citizens - the very people who voted them into power.

Surprisingly, most leaders are afraid to hold people accountable because they do not want to be despised in turn. On the other hand, some leaders cannot hold people accountable especially those who know them well for fear that skeletons in their closets may be exposed.

This may be the reason why corruption goes unchallenged in many workplaces and governments. How can prime ministers send their ministers to jail for embezzling funds when they were doing it together hence making them equally corrupt?

How can a married pastor rebuke a deacon for an extramarital affair when he is going out with his secretary? How can he truly hold him accountable? Will, he not turn a blind eye on the affair lest he is called a hypocrite?

Gifts

Gifts are undeserved things that someone gives you willingly. Gifts can also be defined as God's divine abilities or capacities bestowed on His children to operate like Him.

There are natural gifts or talents that you are born with, then there are spiritual gifts. As children of God it is important for us to realise that God is the source of all our gifts. Gifts come from above. God gives us spiritual gifts and senses as tools to operate in the spiritual realm. Spiritual gifts help us to walk in our purposes.

James 1:16-17 "Do not be deceived my dear brothers and sisters, every good and perfect gift is from above coming down from the father of heavenly lights who does not change like shifting shadows".

There are different types of spiritual gifts namely word of wisdom, word of knowledge, faith, gift of healings, prophecy, miracles, discerning of spirits, tongues and interpretation of tongues.

"For to one is given through the Spirit the utterance of wisdom, and to another the utterance of knowledge according to the same Spirit, to another faith by the same Spirit, to another gifts of healing by the one Spirit, to another the working of miracles, to another prophecy, to another the ability to distinguish between spirits, to another various kinds of tongues, to another the interpretation of tongues (1 Corinthians 12: 8-10).

Paul tells us about other gifts namely serving, teaching, exhortation, leadership, giving and mercy.

"We have different gifts, according to the grace given to each of us. If your gift is prophesying, then prophesy in accordance with your faith; if it is serving, then serve; if it is teaching, then teach, if it is to encourage, then give encouragement; if it is giving, then give generously; if it is to lead, do it diligently; if it is to show mercy, do it cheerfully"
(Romans 12:6-8).

It is important for children of God to know their gifts. If you do not know your gift and your purpose, you need to pray that God reveals it to you. There are some who know their gifts but are not using them. Some have been given to write books, some to write worship songs and some are called to be worshippers. Some are good ushers in church while others do well in various things. Each one needs to find their purpose as part of the body of Christ.

God also blesses His children with blessings for example wealth, children and various talents.

Stewardship

Stewardship simply means taking care of something that is not yours. Biblically stewardship is utilizing and managing all resources God provides for His glory and the betterment of creation.

The Word of God tells us in Psalm 24:1 that *the earth and everything in it belongs to God.* This, therefore, means that all that you and I have belongs to the Lord. When each one of us were born, God had already deposited gifts into our lives. Some people are using their gifts, yet others are sitting on their gifts always giving excuses as to why they are not walking in their calling.

Christians have different gifts for an example speaking in tongues, prophecy, evangelism, teaching, serving, healings, working of miracles and others. Some were called to be Preachers, Prophets, Evangelists, Apostles, and Teachers. Some were anointed to write books, some to worship, some to write worship music and some to be Kingdom Financiers.

Be that as it may, not all these people are using their gifts or walking in their callings. With all these many great gifts you and I have been given stewardship over, comes accountability to God for those gifts.

Myles Munroe once said, "The wealthiest place in the world is not the gold mines of South America or the oil fields of Iraq and Iran. They are not the diamond mines of South Africa or the banks of the world. The

15

wealthiest place on the planet is just down the road. It is the cemetery. There lie buried companies that were never started, inventions that were never made, bestselling books that were never written, and masterpieces that were never painted. In the cemetery is buried the greatest treasure of untapped potential."

When teaching about stewardship Jesus taught the parable of the Talents (in Matthew 25). In the parable a master was going away on a trip and he gave his 3 servants stewardship over his property. To one he gave 5 talents to the other two and to the last one 1 talent. The master must have expected them to make profit because when he came back, he was happy with the servant who he had given five talents as he made five more and the one who had been given two talents made two more talents.

The one who had been given one talent went and hid it and when the master came still had one talent and hence the master was disappointed in him. The master took away the one talent and gave it the one who had 5 talents.

This parable teaches us that we need to be good stewards of what God has put in us as we will individually stand accountable before God.

Because we have been given gifts which we are stewards over, we automatically become answerable to God for those gifts.

Introduction

Since the age of the Internet, many scandals have been exposed in institutions. Most notably, the sexual abuse of young boys by some Catholic priests and the abuse of underage girls by some celebrities. All this abuse went on for years before coming to light. The sad part is the fact that there are people who knew about the abuse when it was taking place but decided to keep quiet.

"Some authors have described the sexual abuse crisis as the biggest crises ever in the Catholic church since the reformation", (Oakley F and Russett B, 2004, p.22)

However, because of the media, the abusers are now being held accountable for what they did decades ago and the abused are now being empowered to stand up and to speak out about the abuse years later. Unfortunately, in some instances, it has taken decades for the victims to get justice and some of them and the perpetrators have since died.

There have also been many scandals of extramarital affairs by people who hold big positions in churches. Because of the media, some have been exposed and some have been swept under the carpet. The church is conforming to the world. In some churches, financial scandals have been exposed while other churches have serious fights about high positions year after year.

Recently, many scandals of corrupt government leaders have been exposed worldwide. Many have become multi-millionaires and siphoned money outside their countries and into their offshore accounts to avoid being caught and for some to evade taxes. Most of them have however not been held accountable for that. Not only has this been happening in Africa, but of late such scandals have been exposed in the western countries too. I strongly believe that if people become bold enough to hold leaders accountable, governments, churches and homes would run more smoothly.

In 2017 the Harvey Weinstein sex scandal gave rise to the exposé of many other Hollywood scandals which had been happening for decades but because of lack of accountability, nobody challenged the abusers despite the fact that many people knew what was happening.

Some of the women were afraid that if they brought up the allegations no one would believe them because of how powerful and popular the abusers were, and others thought they would lose their jobs. Some women, however, were brave enough to tell their experiences of abuse but no one believed them.

However, decades later some abused women were bold enough to expose what they went through resulting in Harvey Weinstein being held accountable for what he did. This gave rise to many women standing up to tell their stories decades later hence the rise of the #METOO movement.

These events in Hollywood have also given rise to abused women in the UK standing up also to tell stories of abuse by people in power for example politicians and celebrities resulting in the abusers being held accountable for their actions. Holding people accountable for their actions will reduce the cases of abuse as future perpetrators know that they will not get away with it.

In 2017 cases of sexual abuse of underage girls by pastors of some churches as well as sexual abuse of underage boys by some pastors of even mega churches were exposed in USA and other countries giving rise to the #Churchtoomovement. #Churchtoo is a movement against sexual harassment and sexual abuse in the church.

Recently, in some African countries, cases of sexual abuse of underage girls by pastors of mega churches have been exposed. Some of these cases have been exposed 20 years later. These cases have taken time to be exposed and even the investigations are being derailed due to bribing of police and the judiciary system by these wealthy pastors. The sad thing is many church leaders will have been aware of the cases of abuse but fail to report them.

Open Vision Concerning Accountability

On the 20th of April 2010, around 7am my husband and I had just woken up. I was laying on the bed ready to start reading my bible. My husband was sitting by the table reading a Christian book. I was wide awake and suddenly I began seeing an open vision.

This was my first time to ever see an open vision. I asked my husband to give me a pen and paper to write what I was seeing and what God was saying to me. In the open vision I was taken to our church, I could see my pastor sitting in the front row of the church and there was someone standing in front of him. There were no other people in the church. Although I couldn't see the person standing in front of the church, I knew it was Jesus. He started speaking and His message was directed to the pastor. He said to the pastor, "X if you love me, feed my flock! X If you love me feed my flock! X if you love me feed my flock!"

After that, I saw on the church projector the word 'Accountability' written in bold capital letters.

Jesus went on to say, "Pastors are accountable to Him for their flock and therefore they have to feed the flock with a balanced word. Just as in the natural, the body needs a balanced diet, the church also needs a balanced diet/ a balanced word... In the natural, proteins are bodybuilding foods which stand for the word which builds the body of Christ/the church. Pastors, therefore, need to preach a gospel that builds the children of God. The church needs to know the true uncompromised gospel that is not watered down in order for it to grow. The word of God tells us, "*You will know the truth and the truth will set you free*" (John 8:32). The truth is found in the word of God. It is the true word of God that will set the people free. Just as lack of proteins causes the body to become malnourished resulting in Kwashiorkor, lack of the true, uncompromised Gospel can cause the church to become spiritually malnourished."

Jesus went on to talk about the natural body needing Vitamins. He said "Vitamins naturally protect the body against diseases, so the church needs to hear the gospel of healing. There is healing in the name of Jesus and through the blood of Jesus. Many pastors teach their churches that miracles and healings were for the early church not for us. This may be because they have not seen healing in their churches and have lost hope. However, this is so wrong as Jesus is the same yesterday today and forever. He never changes. The healing power is operational in these end times more than ever. Christians should have more faith if they are to see miracles in these end times. Miracles, signs and wonders are being experienced and seen in many countries especially in Africa. Pastors need to preach the message of healing and churches should pray that they begin to see healings. More unusual miracles will be seen in these end times. Many incurable diseases will be healed by the blood of Jesus. Is there anything too difficult for God? Jeremiah 32:17 (NIV), says, *"Oh Sovereign God, you have made the heavens and the earth by your great power and outstretched hand. Nothing is too difficult for you"*.

Jesus also spoke about the importance of calcium in the natural which is for strong bones and teeth. The church body needs to be strong enough to stand and not be blown away by the different doctrines in the world today. The church also needs to be strong to withstand shakings. Strength is found in God. Isaiah 40:29 says, *"He gives strength to the weary and increases the power of the weak"*. Habakkuk 3:19 (NIV) says, *" The Sovereign Lord is my strength, he makes my feet like the feet of a deer, he enables to trade on the heights"*.

Carbohydrates and fats provide the body with energy in the natural. The church needs the energy to be vibrant and active. The church cannot afford to be passive, but it needs to go out and win souls for Christ. There are many people who have not been reached by the word and many more who have backslidden. The church should have the energy to go into the community with the gospel and to send missionaries to nations which have not been reached by the gospel.

In the natural, water is very important for the body. This is because many body systems need water in order to function for example the digestive, excretory and circulatory to mention a few. Approximately 60% of the body weight is water. People can rarely survive without water for more than 3 days, but they can survive for a week or so without food. In the bible, water represents the word of God. The body of Christ at large and individual Christians can barely survive spiritually without the word of God. This is why the body of Christ needs the pure, unadulterated word of God.

Jesus went on to say too much of the same nutrient causes the body to be sick. If children keep asking their parents to give them junk food instead of healthy and balanced meals and they end up complying so as not to upset them, the children may end up being sick and obese. Obesity can cause tiredness and laziness resulting in an ineffective and sick church. So, just as in the natural children need to be taught and encouraged to always have balanced meals, the body of Christ needs to be fed with a balanced gospel instead of a watered-down gospel that pricks their ears.

Jesus said pastors are accountable for teaching the church the true gospel. The uncompromised gospel is what the body of Christ needs now when the coming of the Lord Jesus Christ is imminent more than ever before. We are living in the last of the last days. They are only two places people can go to after their death; heaven or hell.

There is no neutral zone so pastors should direct they flock towards heaven. This is why the message of heaven and hell needs to be preached in churches.

The Lord spoke about the need for Christian parents to teach their children the truth of the gospel.

He said parents are accountable for their children, therefore they have to play their part. Parents and pastors should work hand in hand to teach the youth about purity/abstinence, sexuality as well as the dangers of the New Age occults, goths, white witchcraft, satanism and others.

Parents should explain to them how seemingly innocent things like white witchcraft and New Age cause doors to be opened in their lives giving room for demons to enter. God said pastors should also teach their flocks about tithing, fasting, holiness, heaven, hell and most importantly about the Holy Spirit and his gifts instead of preaching the comfy, 'feel good' gospel.

In this decade, more than others, some pastors mostly teach the prosperity gospel. While the prosperity gospel is good, and God wants His children to prosper and be in good health, the prosperity gospel needs to be balanced. Part of the body of Christ is running after riches, they are more concerned about owning the best car in their neighbourhood and owning expensive houses even if it means accruing debt. The word of God clearly tells us what to prioritise which is seeking the kingdom of God; "*Seek ye first the kingdom of God, and his righteousness, and all these things shall be added unto you*" (Matthew 6:33). Do not get me wrong good cars and houses are not bad at all but do not chase after them, they will be added unto you as you seek God. Pastors who do not preach the uncompromised and balanced gospel will stand accountable to God for misleading the flock.

On the other extreme other pastors teach their flock that the rich will not make it into the Kingdom of God and that only the poor will inherit the kingdom of God, yet it is God's desire that His children prosper and be in good health! Such pastors will also stand accountable to God for misleading their flock. Matthew 5:3 says, *"Blessed are the poor in spirit for theirs is the kingdom of heaven."* The word is describing the poor in spirit maybe referring to humility, not financial poverty.

Leaders of Churches:
Apostles, Bishops, Pastors, Evangelists

A lot of church leaders today preach a watered-down gospel, a sugar-coated gospel; a gospel that tickles the ears of the listeners and keeps the flock excited. Pastors are more worried about not offending their church members who may be living in sin and hence they do not preach the truth that will save them.

They fear the truth might offend some members resulting in them leaving the church. In some churches today, members are treated differently depending on how much they contribute financially to the church. In some churches, some rich folks/ heavy givers are left to go on living in sin yet holding high positions in church for fear that addressing their sin may offend them and they may stop tithing or even leave the church.

Let it be however known that if such pastors do not repent, when they stand before God, they will be held accountable for that. In such churches, should people who do not contribute much financially be found in sin they are quickly rebuked and suspended from their leadership roles or singing in the choir when their way of life is exposed. Such people are rebuked in front of the church but not so with the rich folks who go about flaunting their sinful lifestyles knowing very well that the pastor will not dare challenge them but will only tell them 'God understands we are all work in progress'. Really, when some are sleeping around with

26

young girls in church and some ladies cohabiting with their boyfriends! What happened to "go and sin no more" (John 8:11c)

The reason why some pastors look the other side is that 'heavy givers' may be offended and decide not to buy grocery, suits or cars for the pastors. If they are worship leaders or in the worship team who are living in sin, they continue with their duties but if it is someone who does not give much because of lack they are told to step down for a season.

Yes, people can receive Christ and start coming to church still hooked on drugs or sleeping around - they come as they are. However, if 1 or 2 years down the line they are still comfortable in their sinful lifestyle and maybe introducing it to others in the church, then there is something wrong with the gospel being preached.

The gospel has the power to change people's lives. Once they receive Jesus into their lives the Word of God starts to change them. Their minds go through a process of renewal. The word of God says *"And do not be conformed to this world but be ye transformed by the renewal of the mind that you may prove what is good and acceptable and perfect will of God* (Romans 12:2).

Many Christians, however, are being found conforming to the world in every way. Conforming to the world is now being seen as fashionable. It even seems as if churches are competing in conforming to the world in the name of winning more souls to Christ. Friends, do not reduce yourself to a worldly level. You should be saying been there, done that, no turning back!

It should be noted that we are living in the last of the last days. The coming of the Lord is more imminent than ever before. Paul said to Timothy, "*For the time will come when people will not put up with sound doctrine. Instead, to suit their own desires, they will gather around them a great number of teachers to say what their itching ears want to hear. They will turn their ears away from the truth and turn aside to myths. But you, keep your head in all situations, endure hardship, do the work of an evangelist, discharge all the duties of your ministry*" (2 Timothy 4:3-5).

For those men and women of God who have been called into ministry, will you one day on your deathbed be able like Paul to say, "*I have fought the good fight, I have finished the race, I have kept the faith* (2 Timothy 4:7) In all honesty will you be able to say "*Finally, there is laid up for me the crown of righteousness, which the Lord, the righteous Judge, will give to me on that Day, and not to me only but also to all who have loved His appearing*" *(2 Timothy 4:8)* Selah!

Pastors, Bishops, Evangelist, just preach the Word as it is in the bible! Lives of hundreds of thousands of people are in your hands. We are living in the last of the last days. Heaven is real, so is hell. People are dying and heading towards hell yet for many years they sat under the sound of your voice while you preached a sugar-coated or a diluted gospel. Remember Romans 14:12 says, "*And so, each of us will give an*

28

account of ourselves to God." As leaders, you will give an account to God of your sugar coating of the Gospel.

Leaders, you are doubly accountable to God. The word of God says, *"To whom much is given, from him much is required of them"* (Luke 12:48). Teach and preach the word of God in such a manner that your flock will get addicted to the pure unadulterated Word, not the 'feel good' gospel so that they do not get offended when they visit elsewhere and hear a pastor teaching/ preaching about holiness or heaven and hell.

Pastors, why does it not bother you when your youth just hook up with each other/ sleep with each other and end up staying together and having children without getting married? Why are you not teaching the youth about abstinence and purity until marriage? Why do you never speak about holiness to the youth and the church at large? Why do many people in your church get comfortable in getting involved in fornication and adultery? Parents have entrusted you with their teenage children and young adults. Is it that you think talking about abstinence is old fashioned? Is it because you think such teachings may make your youths uncomfortable and they may end up leaving and your numbers will go down? How about your daughter who is doing her first year at university in another town? How would you feel if she comes home to say she is dropping out of college as she is pregnant? You may have taught her well but when she went to university, she went to a church where young adults were never taught about the importance of purity. Sowing and reaping is a biblical principle.

Is it okay for your worship leader to be sleeping around with young members of the congregation and keeps standing up every service and "usher the flock into God's presence?" Pastor, how did you choose your worship leader anyway? Is it because of pure talent? Did you even consider their walk with Christ?

God may seem silent now while he gives you time to put your house in order. Do not however mistake His silence for approval! Remember being a worship leader is important as it ushers people into God's presence. So why do you allow someone who is living in sin to lead worship or even be in the worship team? Worship and just singing are two different things all together so it is not about talent only but about fear of the Lord, it is about being anointed to usher the church into God's presence. Bishop/ Pastor always remember that you are accountable to God for your flock. Imagine what may happen if the rapture happens today and you, your worship leader and half of your congregation are left behind. How will that make you feel? What explanation will you give to those left behind with you?

Giving

Pastors need to preach the balanced gospel even in the area of giving. In most churches giving is being narrowed down to giving the church and the Pastor. God loves the orphans and the widows. He clearly indicates in the word how He deeply cares about them. The Word says of God, "Father to the fatherless, a defender to the widows, is *God in His holy dwelling*" (Psalms 68:5). Caring for widows and orphans is not optional for the body of Christ. There is a blessing that comes with taking care of widows and orphans.

In the churches as well as in the communities there are orphans and widows but are we helping them individually or as a church? During the 12 months of the year, how many months do we set aside to helping widows and orphans financially? Are there no orphans in the church who have been kicked out of schools because of inability to pay fees? If so, what are we doing as a church? Are there no orphans and widows in our communities? If so, what are we doing to bless them as a church and as individuals? James 1:27 says, *"Religion that God our father accepts is this: to look after orphans and widows in their distress and to keep oneself from being polluted by the world"*.

Psalms 82:3 encourages us to *"Defend the weak and the fatherless: to uphold the cause of the poor and the oppressed"*.

Pastors, we need to take care of orphans and widows. Here is Job's take on this:

"If I have denied the desires of the poor
or let the eyes of the widow grow weary,
if I have kept my bread to myself,
not sharing it with the fatherless —
but from my youth, I reared them as a father would,
and from my birth I guided the widow —
if I have seen anyone perishing for lack of clothing,
or the needy without garments,
and their hearts did not bless me
for warming them with the fleece from my sheep,
if I have raised my hand against the fatherless,
knowing that I had influence in court,
then let my arm fall from the shoulder,
let it be broken off at the joint.
For I dreaded destruction from God,
and for fear of his splendor I could not do such
things". (Job 31:16-23).

Pastors, you need to also teach your flock to take care of their relatives. Some do not even take care of their parents yet buy groceries for the Pastors every month. You need to teach the balanced Word which says in 1 Timothy 5:8 *"Anyone who does not provide for their relatives, and especially for their own household, has denied the faith and is worse than an unbeliever"*.

Teach your flock to take care of their parents as blessings also come from parents. They need to realise that their parents will forever be their parents no matter what. How many members of your church are wealthy, yet their parents are living in poverty? Selah!

Praise and Worship

Nowadays in many churches, when you step into the church you are bound to get confused. From outside when you hear the beat during praise and worship you will think you are about to step into the nightclub. They just changed the words, but the beat is straight from a worldly song you have heard before.

When you get into the church that's when you hear words like praise Jesus. Many pastors give the excuse that turning the praise to match the world would attract young adults to church. In other words, you are bringing the world into the church to beef up your numbers. When the New Testament church grew to thousands, do you think they were compromising their praise and the worship?

These days pastors are not only compromising the music but the word also. The church is now excessively loving the world, yet the word of God explicitly warns us not to love the world and the things in it. Some churches have a nightclub in part of the building so that the young adults can invite friends to the nightclub and eventually to church.

What would happen when the rapture happens when the youths are dancing in the church nightclub? Pastors does the word of God not say, *"Do not conform to the pattern of this world but be transformed by the renewing of your mind. Then you will be able to test and approve what God's will is — his good, pleasing and perfect will* (Romans 12:2).

Bishops, Pastors and all leaders, need to go back to the unadulterated Word. Jesus never changes, He is still the same so there is no need to water down or sweeten the gospel. There is a danger of adding unto the word or subtracting from it. Preach the gospel as it is. If the gospel changes every century to suit the generation it no longer remains the gospel it will have turned to history. Proverbs 22: 28 has an exhortation, *"Do not move the ancient landmark [at the boundary of the property] which your fathers have set"*.

Preach the Gospel as it is without changing goal posts. If they are to be saved, they will be saved, we do not need to compromise the word, the praise, the way we dance to suit anyone. It is not worth it!

Brethren let us not love the world to that extent. After all the word of God says, *"Do not love the world [of sin that opposes God and His precepts], nor the things that are in the world. If anyone loves the world, the love of the Father is not in him. For all that is in the world — the lust and sensual craving of the flesh and the lust and longing of the eyes and the boastful pride of life [pretentious confidence in one's resources or in the stability of earthly things] — these do not come from the Father but are from the world. The world is passing away, and with it its lusts [the shameful pursuits and ungodly longings]; but the one who does the will of God and carries out His purposes lives forever "*(1 John 2:15-17). As for the dancing, there is no difference between the nightclub dance and praise dance in many churches. Are we not conforming to this world?

As for the message of heaven and hell, Pastors, why do you not want to teach or preach about such topics? Are you afraid it will make your members uncomfortable and some may leave? Is it perhaps you really do not believe that heaven and hell are real? If not, then why are you not changing your ways and start preaching the true unadulterated gospel of the Kingdom.

As a leader, you owe it your flock/ church members to let them know that heaven and hell are real. Should some decide not to walk according to your teaching, then you have at least done your part and their blood will not be in your hands. A couple of years ago someone asked me whether heaven and hell were real. As I started explaining how real they where I was shocked that one Christian I knew who was there told me not to be too sure about the existence of heaven and hell. I then turned to her and asked her whether she was serious, and she said yes. She told me that she was not sure heaven or hell existed and that she thinks they were just mentioned in the Bible, so people leave in peace and respect one another.

I asked her about her faith and she told me she went to church on Sundays to fellowship with friends and show off her new clothes. That left me really concerned and I was not able to really have time to talk to her as she was my boss and did not want to hear any more.

In these last of the last days, God has raised anointed Prophets all over the world. However, while prophecy is good and is part of the fivefold ministry, over the past decade prophetic churches have mushroomed all over the world especially in Africa. The services are characterised by giving words of knowledge about where people stay, what they are wearing how much money is in their bank and that they are going to be successful etc.

Nothing wrong with that at all but these are just but words of knowledge that should precede the real prophetic words. Some prophets are known to give feel good prophetic words only. Many people get excited when they are told their names and where they live. Prophetic words cannot always be about people suddenly receiving money. The word of God says woe unto you prophets who tell their people peace, peace. Woe unto prophets who say to their flock you are good when they are the opposite. The Word of God says, *"The prophets prophecy lies the priests rule by their own authority and my people love it this way but what will you do in the end?"* (Jeremiah 5:31). Pastor what will you do on Judgement Day - the day when you give an account before God of how you led your flock? Pastors, you owe it to your church members to give them the unadulterated Word. Should some decide not to walk according to your teaching then you have at least done your part and their blood will not be in your hands. If Jesus comes today to rapture his church what do you think will happen to you and your flock?

Celebration of Halloween

Halloween is a day that is celebrated around the world especially in the west by Christians and non-Christians alike. It used to be celebrated 31st October to November 2nd but it is now mostly celebrated on 31st October.

The Druist priest and cults believe that the veil between the dead was dropped and during this period dead souls wonder the earth causing havoc. To appease the dead the cults dressed up like the dead. Bonfires where lit and sacrifices made during this period. Many people commune with the dead during this time. It is celebrated with symbols of death, ghosts, devils and witches. It is believed that the Catholics named the pagan celebration Halloween.

This celebration was renowned by cults and it is common knowledge that this is a pagan celebration. Halloween is filled with darkness. However, many Christians allow their children to celebrate Halloween year after year. They believe it is an innocent celebration, so their children should do what their friends will be doing but what they do not seem to know is that there is nothing innocent about the celebration of Halloween.

Halloween is a demonic celebration and you are letting your children to be exposed to demons. On Halloween day, some Christians take their children to bonfire nights and do apple bobbing at home. You are still celebrating Halloween.

It is important for Christian parents to research on activities their children want to be involved in before letting their children take part. But how can parents and their children know unless they are taught? It is therefore the responsibility of Pastors, Bishops and Apostles to teach their flock about the dangers of participating in Halloween.

Some churches now have their youth participating Halloween only that they wear white clothes not black and they do 'nice things'. Witches celebrate Halloween and feel happy when Christians join in. I believe Christians should not celebrate Halloween based on the verses below.

2 Corinthians 6: 14 *"Be ye not unequally yoked together with unbelievers: for what fellowship hath righteousness with unrighteousness and what communion hath light with darkness?"*

3 John 1:11 *"Dear friend, do not imitate what is evil but what is good. Anyone who does what is good is from God. Anyone who does what is evil has not seen God."*

2 Corinthians 6:17 *"Therefore, come out from among unbelievers, and separate yourselves from them, says the LORD. Don't touch their filthy things, and I will welcome you."*

Some churches have decided to have an alternative celebration. While they think it is okay, they will still be celebrating the day. Changing what you call it does not make it right. Christians should not *Christianise* demonic things just to suit themselves. Some parents also allow their children going into white witchcraft and gothism which are demonic. It is the responsibilities of parents to research and inform their children about the dangers of involvement in such activities.

Accountability of Husbands/Fathers

Husbands are the heads of their families. They have a role in setting the pace not only for their children but also for their wife. However, in this day and age, a lot of husbands are more interested in prioritising their careers and their families come after. They prioritise being excellent at their jobs than becoming excellent husbands and fathers.

For Christian husbands, not being involved in the spiritual growth of their children and wives leaves them exposed to the devil. In '*Man after God's Own Heart*' Jim George said, "Christian marriages are disintegrating at an alarming rate". Children in Christian homes are not receiving the proper training and modeling from their parents. And from my perspective, a major contributor to this tragic slide is a husband and father who is not assuming his God-ordained role as a spiritual leader " (George J, 2002, p88).

If a Christian man steps into his role, the wife and children will be encouraged to grow deeper in the word, thus taking his responsibility as a spiritual leader.

On the other hand, if fathers do not take responsibility as spiritual leaders, children may act crazy with no boundaries at all. Some boys may end up doing drugs and drinking and at times getting involved in gangs because of bad company.

Girls can also do the same as their mothers may not be able to handle the children without the help of their father. At times fathers realise when it's too late - may be faced with a pregnant daughter and a son hooked on drugs. While it may not be easy to deal with teenagers, a man after God's own heart prays for his wife and children. He also asks for wisdom and understanding from God that will help him to be a good husband and father.

If fathers do not rise to the occasion, mothers may end up overwhelmed by playing both roles of mother and father and hence half the time they may be stressed and exhausted. The task of raising children becomes easier when husband and wife are doing it together with a united front.

In these last days, there is an error that is happening in many households. A man was originally created to be the breadwinner. However, in many households, women are now breadwinners. For those who live in the rural areas/countryside, it is the women tilling the lands and engaging in agriculture in order to get money to send their children to school and provide food for the household. Some men live in town not supporting their families while others end up living with second wives there in town.

In the diaspora especially in the western countries, most wives work two or three jobs in order to pay rent and send children to colleges and universities while the husbands who are supposed to be taking care of their family will either not be working or working a few hours a week.

As a result, women may get paid even three times the money the husband gets. That is a great error. Why do wives work harder you may ask...In order to pay bills, buy clothes for their children and pay for their school and college fees yet when they were back in Africa the husbands would work hard and pay for the children's university fees or even private school fees.

The wives know they cannot depend on the husband's salary as it will not be enough to pay college or university fees for their children. Because of reversal of roles some husbands may then accuse their wives for usurping authority and refusing to submit forgetting that they would have relinquished their role as breadwinners. By not working or working a few hours a week while the wives are working 60 or 70 or even 90 hours a week, some wives may end up exhausted and depressed.

Many marriages in the diaspora are breaking down because of reversal of roles. On the other hand, there are faithful men who are working hard and taking care of their families hence when they stand before God one day, He will say well done my good and faithful servant. This error can only be rectified when pastors teach men how to care for their families.

I am encouraged by a man who got born again just a few years ago. He is so much into the word of God. Every night he sits down with his family and listens to teachings from a great teacher, does bible study with his family and they pray together before going to bed.

His family sees him studying the word with the Bible, notebook pen and markers and also listen to teachings while writing notes. Not many Christian husbands can spare time to do bible study let alone pray with their families at the end of each day. He also buys Christian books on the subjects he wants to know more about and reads the books with pen, notebook, and highlighter. That is leading by example.

Extramarital Affairs

When people get married, they make vows to be with each other till death do them part. This makes both parties accountable to each other and to God. However, sometime into the marriage either husband or wife can get involved in extramarital affairs. Some men refuse to be accountable to their wives and end up having "small houses" / second homes - extramarital affairs.

The same thing can happen with some wives. Some husbands end up having a family on the side which their family may end up knowing or may never know about. Despite knowing that they have children outside their marriage, they may even refuse to be accountable and take care of the welfare of those children resulting in them living in poverty.

The only time those children get known officially is when the father dies, and they would have come to pay their last respects to the surprise of the wife, children, and relatives. On the other hand, the husband can end up totally neglecting his official family and start taking care of the side wife and her children.

Whether it is the wife or husband involved in an extramarital affair it is not only the other spouse that is hurt but the children are mostly affected. Husbands need to grow up and be accountable for their actions, so should the wives. Once men step up as breadwinners and love their wives as Christ loves the church then it becomes easier for women to submit and vice versa.

Recently I read an article and saw the documentary about a situation which made me cry. It was about an area in a certain African country where children as young as 12 years were being used as prostitutes by some married men. The children sell their bodies to these men to get money to buy food. They were describing how men in suits driving nice cars park elsewhere and meet them in some place where they have sex with them for £1 or £2.

Honestly, how would the same men feel if another man would do that to their daughters? Would they not even commit murder? Some of the children are AIDS orphans and have to prostitute themselves in order to feed their siblings. Others are orphans who live with distant relatives who sent them out to look for money to buy food.

In the documentary, they were saying most of the men do not want to use condoms as they think they are safe from sexually transmitted diseases as they are young. However, some of the girls were saying they are now already HIV positive. So why would a married man want to expose his wife at home to sexually transmitted diseases especially HIV and AIDS. Where is the accountability?

I have also heard of some men molesting their own daughters for years and threatening them with death should they decide to tell their mother or other relatives.

These are the very fathers who have the responsibility of taking care of their children who are physically and sexually abusing them. The mothers may also be facing abuse from their husbands so much that even if the daughter finally has the guts to inform the mother, she would stop them from repeating it to anyone else. Therefore, the child ends up with nowhere to run and the abuser is empowered even more as there's no one to make him accountable for his actions.

Parents

The Word of God tells us "*that children are gifts from God*" (Psalms 127:3). However, in this age, it is only a few parents who are caring enough to spend quality time with their children to prepare them for their future and help them to deal with challenges they may be facing at school or in college.

According to John Macarthur, "Today's parents tend to be more passive and less involved in their children's lives than any generation in our nation's history. They have turned their children over to artificial, surrogate parents" (Miller J. G and Miller K. G, 2016, p38).

Most children are left sitting in front of the television in the lounge or their bedroom or playing videos games. Instead of parents helping in their children's lives they are letting the television and peers to shape their life. Dr. Cruise Hart said, "If we do not shape up our children, they will be shaped by outside forces that do not care what shape our children are in" (Miller J. G and Miller K. G. 2016, p54).

As parents, you may be refusing to be responsible for how your children are brought up. You become so busy with your work that you have no time to monitor what your children are watching on television and on the internet.

Some young boys end up accessing pornographic channels on television and on their computers in their bedrooms under your nose. You may be working 2 or 3 jobs so your children have comfortable lives but how will it help when you discover your child has become addicted to pornography or drugs under your watch? How will it help when you see the police at your door telling you that your child has been stabbed and you learn they were in a gang or selling drugs? How will it will help when you discover your daughter is pregnant and you realise the people you always left with your children may be responsible?

Parents allow their children to go for sleepovers at houses they have never been to. They do not even know the family where they are taking their child to. How reckless can you become as a parent? What if your child is introduced to sex and drugs at those sleepovers? Who will you blame? Parents need to wake up and understand that we are all living in perilous times.

Do not expect teachers to play a parental role to your children. Children of today are not as innocent as their parents were 20-30 years ago at their age. Technology has introduced good as well as bad things to our children. Some parents are not even concerned that their 13-year-old child is on social media. You have not taught them the dangers of social media.

There are men out there pretending to be 15-year-olds using profile pictures of younger boys and befriending children on social media platforms and planning to meet them for a drink somewhere.

Parents need to be accountable for their children. Refuse to let peer pressure, television, or social media mould your children. Children are hungry for knowledge, and when they have reached puberty, they may have many questions.

Frank Roosevelt once said, "We may not be able to prepare the future for our children, but we can at least prepare our children for the future" (Miller J.G and Miller K.G, 2016, p 113). As parents, you need to take time with them to explain what is happening in their bodies and how to respond to it.

Do not leave everything to the teachers to explain to your children when you are busy making money. Your children do not need to end up googling answers to questions about life because when you come home you are working in the study on your computer and do not want to be disturbed. Be reminded that one day you will give an account of how you raised your children before the Almighty.

God has made you stewards of those children. The word of God says, *"Moreover it required of stewards that they may be found faithful"* (1 Corinthians 4:2 ESV). As parents, you need to be role models for your children. "Modelling is the most powerful of all teachers", (Miller J.G and Miller K.G, 2016, p.81). Unfortunately, many parents tend to look outside their families for role models for example celebrities, teachers and other relatives.

As parents, you should teach your children to be accountable from a tender age. Children cannot be accountable when their parents are not. Accountable parents are bound to raise accountable children. No matter how busy and how difficult it may be as parents, you should balance your time and spend time with your children.

Children should be prioritised over many things. Some parents give their children a lot of money and think that will help. However, money can never replace time with your children. "In bringing up children spend on them half as much money and twice as much time" (Miller J.G and Miller K.G, 2016, p 50).

Training up a child is a parental responsibility! The word of God says to parents "*Train up a child in the way that he should go, and when he is old he will not depart from it*" (Proverbs 22:6).

Fathers and Their Sons

Fathers, you ought to spend quality time with your sons talking about life. The boys should feel free to open up to their dads about what will be transpiring in their lives as well as ask questions. It is the fathers who should teach their sons the importance of respecting other people.

As they develop from boys to young men, boys need their dads to teach them about how to relate with girls/women and about how to love them so that they will know how to treat a woman with respect when they start dating.

If fathers are not exemplary they should not be surprised when their sons become wild or turn out to be just like them. Fathers should teach their sons how to be gentlemen, how to provide for their families and how to be faithful and trustworthy.

They can also teach their sons how to love their mothers and treat them with respect and also teach the sons how to love and treat their girlfriends /wife.

There are somethings that cannot be *googled.*

Mothers and Their Daughters

Mothers ought to prepare their daughters to be women and to be ready for the future. They should play the role of moulding their daughters to become exemplary future role models. They should teach their daughters domestic chores and responsibility that comes with being a wife and a mother.

By the time daughters leave home they should be able to stand on their own. Mothers, you ought to spend time with your daughters. You should cook with your daughters, teaching them life skills together with your sons.

Some mothers have always had maids and gardeners, so their children would end up not doing any chores at all - that is not doing them any favours.

The daughter's marriage may struggle or end up in divorce if she ends up getting married and cannot cook or clean the house.

On the other end, fathers should teach their daughters how to be wives and how to relate to a man/husband.

Parents and the Power of the Tongue

Many parents use their tongues recklessly when talking to their children especially when they are upset by their actions. However, some do not realise that the tongue has the power to create/ build or destroy lives. I have heard a mother respond many times to her daughter's request for money to buy something as "the way you love money will cause you to become a prostitute when you grow up." That mother used to say it over and over again. That daughter grew up to fulfil her mother's declarations.

Some parents will say to their daughters, "You will never get married" whilst some fathers will say to their sons, "You are not going to be successful" or "You are a good for nothing kid" etc.

I don't know what negative words you have thrown into your children's lives, but I encourage you to nullify those words and start blessing your children instead of cursing them. God desires that we speak life into the lives of our children. Words are powerful. God did not create the heaven and the earth with tangible things but with words.

The word of God says in Proverbs 18:20-21, "*A man's belly shall be satisfied with the fruit of his mouth and with the increase of his lips shall he be satisfied.*

Death and life are in the power of the tongue and they that love it shall eat of the fruit thereof'.

When kids fail in life parents will be quick to blame the devil, God and other people but won't revisit the words that they have sown into their children's lives. Your children will become the product of the words you speak into their lives.

It is not too late, if you used to say terrible things into your children's lives start speaking positively into their lives. Tell them they are talented, successful and they will have great jobs in the future. Look at the areas they are good at and start encouraging them in those areas. Remember you are accountable to God for those children.

As husband and wife, you also need to speak right concerning your marriage and your life. Stop always saying we will never succeed, we will die poor etc. Start declaring you have a good marriage that you have awesome kids and you are super blessed.

Start declaring what you desire to see in your marriage, in your family and in all your children's lives. Even when your marriage seems to be on the rocks 'you need to speak into it.'

In Ezekiel 38, God asks prophet Ezekiel whether there was a chance that the dry bones could live again. God then instructed Ezekiel to speak/prophecy to the dry bones and lo and behold the dry bones lived. Whatever dry bone situation you may be facing with your children, your marriage, your business or your health; speak/prophecy to the situation. It might be difficult to speak things that seem impossible, but you have to ask the Holy Spirit to help you see things as God sees them and start speaking life into your situation.

The Holy Spirit will then tame your tongue to speak victory, joy, abundance, success and good health into your life and the lives of your children. Remember God's promises are Yes and Amen.

Pastors and Church Leaders

Church leaders include Bishops, Apostles, Prophets, Pastors, Elders, Deacons and trustees etc. All church leaders are accountable to God over how they lead their flock. If God gave you a gift or if you have a role in the church, you are accountable to God for how you use your gift. The word of God says, *"For everyone who has been given much, much will be demanded and from the one who has been entrusted with much, much more will be asked"* (Luke 12:48b).

As servants of God, you are accountable for the knowledge, the abilities, the gifts and the resources God has blessed you with. Nowadays, people in churches have itching ears. There are particular messages they get excited about. The word of God tells us, *"For the time will come when people will not put up with sound doctrine, instead to suit their own desires, they will gather around themselves a great number of teachers to say what their itching ears want to hear"* (2 Timothy 4:3).

Some Christians have a feel-good kind of gospel that they prefer to hear. Only a few leaders still preach and teach about sin, holiness, the cross, the blood of Jesus, repentance, heaven or hell. Why is that so you may wonder?

Well, some preachers fear to become unpopular and are worried that their big tithers who may be living in sin may be offended by the messages and perchance stop giving or even leave the church.

Well I have news for you leaders! You are accountable to God and therefore one day you will stand before Him - just you and Him and give an account of how you used your gift and how and what you preached. Romans 14:12 says, "*So then each of us will give an account of ourselves to God*".

Hear me, Pastors, prosperity teaching is good - God wants His children to prosper and be in health but there is more to the Gospel than that. People need to hear a wholesome gospel. They need a balanced gospel. Your job is to feed your flock with a balanced gospel, not junk food (feel good kind of gospel) daily. The flock will end up spiritually malnourished.

When one is born again, they can only be oppressed but not possessed by demons. But listen, some of your church members are born again but are still living in sin. In so doing they open doors to demons. Some of your church members are sleeping around while others have tried some occultic stuff.

If people do that, being born again cannot stop demons coming into their lives. The devil and demons are real. There are times when people need deliverance because they have opened doors to demons by living in sin. Some born again church members may be living as husband and wife without getting married.

Leaders should be bold enough to tell their members that it is wrong, and they need to get married. The more pastors let that happen even the upcoming young men and women in church will think it is right to just live as partners and hence weddings in the church become rare.

Pastors should encourage young adults to keep themselves pure until marriage. If they mess up God will still forgive them, and they can keep running their race but at least you as a pastor will have taught them how to live a life of holiness.

What will you say when you stand before God pastor and He asks you to give an account of the work that you did in leading the flock? How about when Jesus comes and raptures the church, how many members of your church do you think will be caught up in the clouds with Him?

How about you? If by some chance you are left behind with some of your church members you have spent years feeding with the feel-good message, what will you say to them when they ask you why they were left behind. Selah.

There are pastors who teach and preach against healing and speaking in tongues. They say these ended during the New Testament time and are no longer applicable. Then there are those who preach against tithing and as a result rob their flock of God's blessings upon their lives. Also, what happened to teaching the church about going out to win souls? The word of God should be preached as it is. Men and women of God should never forget that they will one day stand before the Lord and give an account of their work before God.

Nowadays it is difficult to distinguish between the church and the world. Church members are dressing the same as going to nightclubs and the music being played in the church is similar to the worldly music. Some songs are taken from the world and played in church as they are. In other circumstances, the rhythm is from the nightclub the difference is just the words. In some cases, the language on the pulpit is straight from the world. May the fear/reverence of the Lord fill the children of God.

Leaders of Nations

Leaders of nations be they presidents, prime ministers, ministers and leaders of political parties are accountable to the citizens who voted them into power but most of all, they are accountable to God.

They are accountable for how they run their nations and how they use the nation's resources especially money. They are also accountable to God for the legislations they enforce. The laws should be in line with God's word especially if the nation happens to be a Christian one.

Citizens should be free to question the government on developmental and economic issues. They also should have a right to confront/challenge the government on corruption. We have seen many African countries that have been run to the ground by corruption. Some countries have had serious corruption issues and of late corruption has been exposed in European countries too.

Corrupt leaders refuse to be accountable to the very citizens who voted them into power. In a certain African country, cabinet ministers who do not officially earn much have been seen to build mansions, have multiple expensive cars and live luxurious lives while ordinary citizens are living in poverty.

Where they got the money from is every citizen's guess. However, because they are equally corrupt, presidents and prime ministers cannot hold them accountable as they know how corrupt they each are. Some presidents and their ministers have offshore accounts and they steal millions of dollars from their countries and have houses all over the world while their citizens are literary living in poverty.

Many scandals go unchallenged because each one has their own scandal that is well known in their circles. Citizens are robbed of their right to protest. Many end up in jail for peaceful demonstrations. Fear makes the citizens afraid of holding the government accountable. However democratic nations should give their citizens their right to protest or hold them accountable.

Elections in African and some western countries are rigged. Some parties can be in power for decades by rigging elections. Leaders refuse to be accountable to their citizens and other nations but there is one who sees everything. Such leaders will one day stand accountable to God Himself.

However, if a nation is run by leaders with integrity they will make themselves accountable to each other and to the citizens. They will also not hesitate to challenge corruption and bring people to book. Presidents and their cabinet come up with laws and legislation that help to run the nation and make it successful. They should come up with legislation that shows integrity and the love and fear of the Lord. As corrupt people are brought to book their assets should be ceased and they should be made to pay back stolen money which will be used for the good of the nation.

The church has to rise up and help the government leaders to come up with legislation that is in line with God's word. It is the duty of the church to pray for their governments. Leaders of nations are accountable to God for all the ungodly legislation they enforce.

Personal Accountability

Wherever we are, whatever we do we have to be accountable people. Some people tend to associate accountability with stress and punishment, but it is more about being responsible.

In workplaces where there are no clear-cut expectations, employees are bound not to work at their best but just do minimal. In such cases there is no professional accountability. However, in companies where there are clear cut expectations and where employees know they are held accountable for their work the companies succeed.

However, as Christians we should do our best in everything that we do and work as unto God. In my workplace I do a lot of lone working. I have told myself I work as unto God. I do not work to please anyone but God. If I work to please my Supervisor or Manager, there are not with me most of the time hence I would end up doing minimal work.

In many workplaces, some people are known to be late all the time. Others are well known to extend their breaks. Some employees are known to fake sickness. I was talking to a friend who was complaining that at her workplace there are people who are well known to fake sickness all the time and there are others who are always late for work, but the managers never hold them accountable.

She said the most annoying thing is a few of those people are Christians. My friend was actually frustrated but what she said impressed me. She told me she will never lower herself to their level and fake sickness or go to work late.

As a Christian, even if your managers do not hold you accountable for how you work, God will one day hold you accountable for how you performed at work. Why, you might ask? Because you are God's ambassador at your workplace. If people know you as someone who shouts at others at work, uses swear words and is always complaining how do you think your workmates will feel about Christianity? You need to examine yourself and make some changes. Be a better person and employee.

A couple of years when I was on attachment, I worked in a nursing home. As we were trying to manoeuvre the hoist around to move a patient I knocked over and broke the patient's perfume bottle that was half full. The patient had dementia. I apologised to the patient and she said it was okay, it was an accident. My colleague helped me clear the mess. When we had finished, I told my colleague I was going to report the incident to the Deputy Manager, and I was going to record the incident. My colleague told me it was not necessary as we had cleared the 'evidence' and no one would know it was us.

Because I always endeavour to work as unto God I insisted on recording and went and told my Deputy. She thanked me for my honesty.

I told her I was going to replace the perfume bottle of which she insisted it was not necessary as the patient had said it was okay. It took me a whole week to find the perfume as shops no longer stocked it. I finally found it online. Though most people were selling it for about £15, I found a website that had a huge perfume sale and was selling it in box sets for £6. I bought several box sets, sold some at double the price and gave the patient her full bottle. When I told my Deputy Manager that I had replaced the perfume bottle she was surprised and commended me for that.

Another time while at work, I went to the shop at break time to buy a few bits. (The shop was a distance from my workplace). When I got my change, I just put it in my coat pocket. When I got back to my colleagues, I found out I had been given £10 more in change. When I told my colleagues that I was going back to the shop with the extra money, they actually shouted at me and said "Who does that! It's your 'blessing' from God just take it or if don't want it give it to us."

Long story short, I took it back. Despite being shouted at by the shop keeper who assumed I had come back to say he had short changed me, I just told him on the contrary you gave me £10 more and just gave him the money and left him almost in shock.

What would you do? And what would you do if you see somebody dropped their purse and you opened it and realise it has a lot of money and nobody has seen you and the owner of the purse is oblivious of the fact that they have lost their purse.

Remember, one day you will stand before God and give an account for that action should you choose to steal the money in the purse.

Last week I was reading an article on social media and people were commenting on the article. I was surprised that the person received so many negative comments but what really shocked me most was a lady whose negative comment was full of unbelievable obscenities especially that she even used obscenities to refer to the writer as a "son of a whore".

Out of curiosity I went on the lady's profile and was shocked that she indicated on her profile that she is Christian, she loves the Lord and she is a praying woman. Her profile was full of bible verses.

Friends, we need to know that one day we will each stand before God and give an account of our lives to Him.

"I tell you, on the Day of Judgment people will give account for every careless word they speak, for by your words you will be justified, and by your words you will be condemned." (Matthew 12:36-37).

In this decade more than ever, many Christians are getting caught up in extra marital affairs. The sad thing is that it's not only just ordinary Christians but leaders of churches too. Some leaders even dare find verses to justify their adulterous affairs. Christians should lead exemplary lives instead of conforming to the world. Each and every one of us will stand before God and give an account of our lives so we have to live holy lives.

Forgiveness

As we live our lives, we are bound to face offenses every day. Jesus told his disciples that it is impossible but that offences will come (Luke 17:1). Because we will face offenses, it is important to learn to forgive.

Forgiveness simply means to cease to blame or to hold resentment against someone. For Christians, forgiveness is a command from God not an option. Be that as it may so many Christians are living with unforgiveness and bitterness, some will even declare that they will never forgive whoever offended them because they hurt them very much.

Matthew 6:15 says, "But if you refuse to forgive others, your father will not forgive you of you sins". I am sure if you die with your sins not forgiven by your Father you may not make it to heaven. Sin simply means missing the mark, which is the standard of perfection set by God and obviously unforgiveness is a sin.

The question is whether it is worth it for you to keep the unforgiveness or bitterness? I personally do not think you want to go to church for twenty or thirty years and at the end of it all die and go to hell because you refused to forgive your husband who cheated on you or your friend who gossiped behind your back.

Forgiveness does not mean condoning sin or excusing sin but is making sure someone's wrong doing does not affect you physically or emotionally.

Unforgiveness may affect your health and you may end up having stress, heart problems and high blood pressure.

Some Christians will say I need a year to forgive my friend. What if you have less than a year to live? What will you say when you stand before God and He asked you to give an account of your life?

Some Christians will ask why they should forgive. This is because forgiveness is not an option but a command, also because if you do not forgive God will not forgive you. Lastly forgiving someone will improve your physical health. You will have no more stress and no high blood pressure.

I encourage you to examine your life to see whether you have unforgiveness or bitterness in your life if so, ask the Holy Spirit to help you to forgive.

Accountability Partners

An accountability partner is a person you are in collaboration with who will help you to succeed and hold you accountable for your dreams and aspirations. It is someone who will hold you accountable for what you will do or say.

A couple of years ago well after God had talked to me about accountability and I came across a message on accountability partners. I knew that I really needed an accountability partner in my life. My best friend and cousin Patience happens to be my prayer partner also and to a certain extent, she has always played the role of an accountability partner to me well before I even knew about accountability partners.

When I researched into accountability partners, I asked her to be my accountability partner and after praying about it we officially became accountability partners. I believe you can have one accountability partner, but you can always have a group of Christian friends or even two that you can be accountable to.

Accountability is key in relationships. If you are to succeed in what you do you cannot make it on your own. You need someone to push you and encourage you to be your best. You see, there are qualities that an accountability partner should hold. They should be a good listener, a person who values confidentiality, a person who has the fear of God in them as well as being a praying person. "In essence, an accountable man is a Christian who is willing to risk opening his life to others in order to become answerable for his attitudes and actions" (Eisenman T.L, 2004, p.17).

If one is not free to open their life to the one that they want to be an accountability partner with, then the partnership will not work. Transparency is key in this relationship so is trustworthiness.

An accountability partner is willing to help you and push you along the way if need be. It is someone who is bold enough to tell you when you are wrong and applaud you when you do well. It is someone who will hold you accountable for what you do and say, someone who calls a spade a spade and who will correct you in love.

"There are essential ingredients that will determine whether accountability works or fails. Without bringing honesty, vulnerability, and teachability to the table, for instance, accountability cannot possibly achieve the spiritual growth and health we seek" (Eisenman T.L, 2004, p.55).

When I have done something wrong my accountability partner does not hesitate to correct me in love. I may not necessarily like it, I may sulk but at the end of the day I will take the correction and rectify what has to be rectified. If my accountability partner tells me I owe a certain person an apology I may think I do not think so, I may take a few days struggling with it, but I will do it. Besides speaking to me through His word and through the still small voice, I know God speaks to me through my accountability partner, so I take heed to what she is telling me, it has to be biblical though.

My accountability partner and I pray for each other and we always talk to see how each of us are doing. When I have been overwhelmed by challenges, my accountability partner has helped me manoeuvre around the challenges.

Recently I lost my mum and despite the fact that God gave me peace that surpasses all understanding after losing my mum, I started having problems in concentrating in reading the word and at times with sleeping. My accountability partner was there for me to comfort and encourage me. When she has her challenges, I also stand with her and in so doing we help each other succeed in all we do.

My accountability partner also checks on how I am doing when I am facing challenges. I do the same with her. We always encourage each other to lead lives that are pleasing unto God and to keep an intimate relationship with God. Not only Christians need an accountability partner. Everyone needs someone who can tell them you are walking on slippery ground or if you keep going that way you will destroy your marriage or just someone who can encourage them in times of challenges. I encourage you to look for an accountability partner if you do not already have one.

Your accountability partner will help you get up when you fall into sin. James 5: 16 says, *"Confess your faults one to another and pray one for another that ye may be healed. The effectual fervent prayers of a righteous man availeth much."*

One of the qualities an accountability partner should have is trustworthiness. Where there is trust it is easy for partners to open up to each other and confess of their faults/sins. Without having an accountability partner, one can just bury their sins and sink in them.

Conclusion

Whether you are a Pastor, Bishop, Sunday School Teacher, Worship Leader or just a church member, just remember one day you will stand before God and give an account of your life. You will give an account of your actions, what came out of your mouth and what you did or did not do. Some people have been asked to write songs, write books, serve as ushers, be encouragers but keep putting it off.

Be assured you will stand before God and give an account of that. Even if you do not believe in God you will one day be face to face with him to give an account of how you lived your life. Be reminded of Romans 14.12 which says, *"And so, each of us must give an account of ourselves to God."*

Whether you really did whatever you did as unto the Lord will be determined by God himself. If Men and Women of God sugarcoat the gospel they will have blood on their hands as they will lead many people to hell. Paul preached the uncompromised gospel.

Pastor, Bishop, Evangelist, Prophet when you are on your death bed, will you be able like Paul to say, I am innocent of the blood of any of you? I will leave you to ponder on the following words below said by Paul:

"Now I know that none of you among whom I have gone about preaching the kingdom will ever see me again. Therefore, I declare to you today that I am innocent of the blood of any of you. For I have not

hesitated to proclaim to you the whole will of God. Keep watch over yourselves and all the flock of which the Holy Spirit has made you overseers. Be shepherds of the church of God,[a] which he bought with his own blood.[b] I know that after I leave, savage wolves will come in among you and will not spare the flock. Even from your own number men will arise and distort the truth in order to draw away disciples after them. So be on your guard! Remember that for three years I never stopped warning each of you night and day with tears. "Now I commit you to God and to the word of his grace, which can build you up and give you an inheritance among all those who are sanctified. I have not coveted anyone's silver or gold or clothing. You yourselves know that these hands of mine have supplied my own needs and the needs of my companions. In everything I did, I showed you that by this kind of hard work we must help the weak, remembering the words the Lord Jesus himself said: 'It is more blessed to give than to receive." (Acts 20:25-35)

Leaders of nations, you will stand accountable to God for legislation that you allowed which is contrary to the Word of God. You will also stand accountable to God for innocent people that have been killed under your watch. Legislators will stand accountable for legalizing abortion on demand even up until the day of birth. Some legislators will stand accountable for banning prayer in public school, removal of bibles in schools, hospitals and hotels and quite recently the call to ban prayers before meetings in UK.

Corrupt leaders of nations and companies who are embezzling money from their governments whilst their citizens are literally living in poverty will stand accountable to God for their actions.

Corrupt Judges who are bribed into sending innocent people to jail, you will stand accountable to God for your actions. I know of many people in the Diaspora who have sent their hard-earned money to friends and relatives to help them build or buy houses and their money has been squandered even by Christians. Some of those people got loans from banks to finance the projects and most are now going through depression as they have to continue paying back the money to their banks, yet they got nothing out of it as the money was used to sponsor luxury lifestyles.

Leaders of churches who are sexually abusing under age children and other members of their flock will stand accountable to God! Leaders of churches who are abusing church finances should repent or perish. They too will stand accountable before God. Also, those preachers and prophets who are selling the gospel as well as selling prophecy will stand accountable before God. The fact that God has not done anything as yet does not mean he approves but he is giving you a chance to repent servant of God!

Our God is a God of justice! The people who were entrusted with the money and abused it will stand accountable to God. Socrates, the Philosopher, once said, "An unexamined life is not worth living" so, let us take time to examine our lives and repent as well as rectify areas that need to be rectified.

For those who work let us continue to do the best at our jobs for the good of our companies. Those who are Christians work as unto the Lord, be known to be the best worker who is faithful and can be trusted by your bosses, not because you want a promotion but because that is the right thing to do.

Do not be the one who causes bosses to say they do not want to promote Christians because they are lazy but be the opposite. Instead do your job heartily as unto the Lord. As for those Christians who are still holding unforgiveness and bitterness in their hearts, I encourage you to ask the Holy Spirit to help you to forgive and release whoever offended you.

Friends, we should honour God in everything we do. Before you do something that you are not comfortable with ask yourself whether that action honours God. The word of God says, "A son honours his father, and a slave honours his master. If I am a father where is the honour due to me?" If I am a master where is the respect due to me?" says the Lord Almighty (Malachi 1:6).

At the end of the day we should all remember Romans 14:12 which says, *"And so, each of us must give an account of ourselves to God."*

Bibliography

1. Business dictionary.com
2. Eisenman T.L. (2004), *The Accountable Man*, (IVP Books: Illinois)
3. George, J. (2002), *Man After God's Heart*, (Harvest House Publishers: Eugene, Oregon
4. Miller J. G. and Miller K. G, (2016) *Raising Accountable children*, (Penguin group: USA)
5. Merrimack Webster dictionary
6. Oakley F. and Russett B. (2004), *Governance, Accountability and Future of the Catholic Church*, (Continuum Publishers: New York).

To contact author:
nzphiri@gmail.com
prayers3am@yahoo.co.uk